A Little German Cookbook

Gertrud Philipine Matthes

ILLUSTRATED BY RUTH BLEAKLEY-THIESSEN

First published in 1990 by
The Appletree Press Ltd, 7 James Street South,
Belfast BT2 8DL. Text © Gertrud Philipine Matthes, 1990.
Illustrations © Ruth Bleakley-Thiessen, 1990.
Printed in the U.K. All rights reserved.

British Library Cataloguing in Publication Data
Matthes, Gertrud Philipine
A little German cookbook.
I. Food: German dishes – Recipes
I. Title
641.5943

ISBN 0-86281-238-0

First published in the United States in 1990 by
Chronicle Books, 275 Fifth Street, San Francisco,
California 94103.

ISBN 0-87701-736-0

9 8 7 6 5 4 3 2 1

Introduction

Visitors to Germany leave with memories of hearty, delicious yet simple meals. Traditions and folklore are important to German culture, and numerous festivals and religious holidays are celebrated annually. On these occasions age-old recipes are still used. Restaurants and inns are proud of their specialities, which are reminiscent of the simple, home-cooked family meals once prepared by grandmother. The recipes in this book come from all parts of Germany – north, south, east and west. Germans have hefty appetites for good food and this book contains a selection of popular recipes to tempt even the most diet-conscious, together with cakes and traditional Christmas fare. The dishes are easy to prepare, and are practical, economical and good.

Enjoy yourself, and *Guten Appetit!*

A note on measures

Metric, imperial and volume measurements have been given for all the recipes. For perfect results use one set only. Metric measures should be used where no American measure is shown, as for meat weights. Spoon measurements are level except where otherwise indicated. Seasonings can of course be adjusted according to taste. Recipes are for four.

Frühstück

Breakfast

The basically simple German breakfast becomes special as you sit down to a mini-feast of steaming hot, aromatic coffee, accompanied by a variety of crisp rolls straight out of the oven.

There is always an early riser who is willing to collect these from the nearest bakery (there are over 200 different kinds of bread and a great many types of rolls to choose from). Creamy butter, homemade jam and honey usually complete the menu, but in most hotels today breakfast includes a Wurst (cold meat) platter, boiled eggs and even an assortment of cakes.

Of all the various ways of making good coffee I think the filter method is best. It is of course important that you buy freshly roasted beans. Choose your favourite blend and grind them down to a fine powder to ensure maximum flavour (allow I heaped teaspoon per cup). Filter it straight into your coffee-pot or use an electric coffee-maker. To really bring out the character of your selection add a pinch of salt to the finished brew. Serve it straightaway, white or black, and never reheat it.

Leberklösschensuppe

Liver Dumpling Soup

Soups have always been important in Germany. As they are usually filling and satisfying, they could easily be served on their own as a light lunch or supper. This is a favourite of my mother's. For the stock you could use stock cubes, but they are a poor substitute.

Stock
1 litre/2 pt/5 cups water
250 g/8 oz stewing meat, or either marrow bones or chicken bones
2 sticks celery, 2 leeks, 2 carrots, 1 onion, parsley stalks
salt and pepper

Place meat or bones with the water into a pot, cover and boil for 1 hour. Chop the vegetables, add to liquid and boil for a further hour. Season and strain keeping only the clear stock.

Dumplings

1 stale bread roll	*1 tbsp parsley*
milk	*1 egg*
100 g/4 oz goose liver	*2 rashers streaky bacon*
(or any other)	*salt*
1 tbsp chopped onion	*marjoram*

Dumplings Soak the bread roll in milk and squeeze out, mince it and the other ingredients and form a paste. Form teaspoon-size ovals, and drop gently into boiling stock and simmer for 10 minutes. Serve hot, garnished with chopped chives.

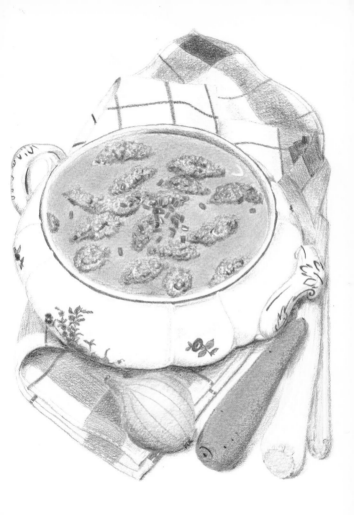

Flädchensuppe

Pancake Soup

This is another of my mother's favourite recipes for soup.

---

50 g/2 oz/½ cup plain flour
1 egg
150 ml/¼ pt/½ cup milk
½ tsp salt
lard for frying
1 litre/2 pt/4 cups stock (see page 6)
chives (for garnish)

Whisk flour, egg, milk and salt into a smooth batter. Heat a little lard in a frying-pan, pour in some of the batter and fry on both sides until golden brown. Repeat until the batter is used up.

Cut pancakes into small strips and add to simmering stock. Remove from heat and let the soup stand for about 5 minutes. Garnish with chopped chives and serve hot.

Himmel und Erde

Heaven and Earth

This light and tasty meal from Westphalia takes its name from the ingredients used, potatoes representing Earth and the fluffy layers of apples Heaven.

1½ kg/3 lb potatoes	vinegar
1 kg/2 lb apples	4 rashers bacon
salt	1 onion (sliced into rings)
sugar	

Peel and dice potatoes and apples. Boil them separately in salted water till tender. Drain and add a little salt, sugar and vinegar to taste. Put alternate layers of potatoes and apples into serving dish and keep hot. Dice the bacon and fry with the onion rings until crisp, and use as garnish.

Leipziger Allerlei

A Leipzig Medley

Originating from Saxony, this mixture of baby vegetables is an appetising accompaniment to lamb or veal, or it can make an attractive lunch on its own.

250 g/8 oz of each of the following: peas, small whole carrots, asparagus (cut into short pieces)	
1 sliced kohlrabi	
1 small cauliflower (separated into florets)	
150 ml/¼ pt/½ cup stock	a little water
50 g/2 oz/4 tbsp butter	salt
1 tsp cornflour	sugar

For best results use young, juicy vegetables. Fry lightly in butter, add the stock, cover the pot and simmer until tender (about 25 minutes). Mix cornflour with enough water to make a paste and stir it into the vegetables. Simmer for a further 5 minutes. Season to taste and serve.

Quark mit Kümmel und Pellkartoffeln

Cream Cheese with Caraway Seeds and Baked Potatoes

This is an easy 'Friday night' meal . . . when the week's work is done. It is economical and delicious too.

1 kg/2 lb small potatoes	250 g/8 oz/2 cups cream
caraway seeds (to taste)	cheese
salt	2-3 tbsp milk or cream
25 g/1 oz/2 tbsp butter	chives, chopped

Clean potatoes but do not peel. Cut in half, dip the cut side into the caraway seeds and salt, place on a well-greased baking sheet with the seeded side uppermost and cook in oven at medium heat (gas mark 4/350°F/180°C) until soft (about 30 minutes). Brush with melted butter. Mix the cheese with milk or cream. Add a pinch of salt and chopped chives. Serve with the potatoes in a separate dish.

Heringe in saurer Sahne

Herrings in Sour Cream

This recipe for the humble herring is simply delicious with rye bread or baked potatoes as a light meal, or, as an hors d'oeuvre, arranged on a bed of lettuce.

4 rollmop herrings	1 small apple, diced
300 ml/½ pt/1 cup sour cream	2 tsp wine vinegar or lemon juice
1 small onion, finely sliced	salt and pepper

Cut herrings into small strips. Mix together cream, onion, apple and vinegar, and pour over herrings. Season to taste. Leave to stand for 3 hours before serving.

But remember, 'Fish, like a guest, will stink after 3 days.'

Kabeljau mit Pilsen

Cod with Mushrooms

In Germany, fish is sometimes regarded as a distinctive meal to be served with elaborate sauces on special occasions. This recipe is simple yet has a certain piquancy.

1 kg/2½ lb fresh cod	1 parsnip
juice of 1 lemon	250 g/8 oz mushrooms
peppercorns	150 ml/¼ pt/½ cup white wine
2 bay leaves	
1 stick celery	salt
1 leek	1 tbsp butter

Clean the fish and rub in the lemon juice. Place it in a casserole with the peppercorns and bay leaves, and let it stand for 30 minutes. Blanch the thinly sliced celery, leek and parsnip and place with sliced mushrooms around the fish. Season and pour over the wine, dot with butter, cover with foil and bake in oven for 50 minutes at gas mark 4/350°F/180°C.

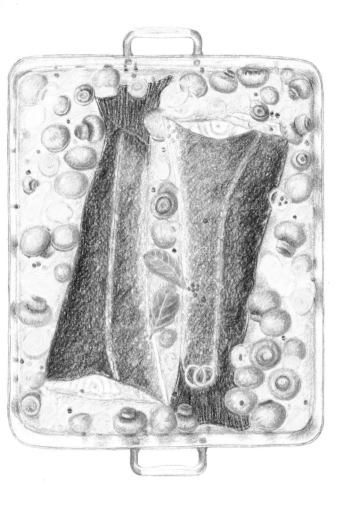

Kartoffelpuffer mit Preiselbeeren

Potato Cakes with Cranberries

This is a very old, traditional supper dish, loved by everyone I know. Serve these pancakes with stewed fruit or a green salad and eat them as soon as they come out of the pan. I like them best with stewed cranberries, but North Germans prefer them with sliced, cooked apple.

1 kg/2½ lb raw potatoes	25 g/1 oz/2 tbsp flour or
salt	breadcrumbs
1 small onion	100 g/4 oz/8 tbsp lard or oil
2 eggs	

Peel the potatoes and grate finely. Mix in salt, grated onion, eggs and flour or breadcrumbs. Heat the fat in a frying pan, drop in the mixture in spoonfuls and flatten with a spatula. Fry on both sides till crisp and golden brown.

Sauerbraten

Beef in Marinade

This must be the most popular meat dish in Germany. Many's the time I've ordered Sauerbraten only to be told by the waiter 'That's off'!

---

1 kg/2½ lb sirloin beef

For the Marinade

1 onion	300 ml/½ pt/ 1 cup wine
4 peppercorns	vinegar
2 cloves	375 ml/13 fl oz/1¼ cups
1 bay leaf	water

For Braising

60 g/3 oz/5 tbsp fat	1 crust rye bread
salt	2 tsp cornflour
600 ml/1 pt/2 cups water	1 tbsp cold water

Place beef in earthenware bowl with thinly sliced onion rings. Add spices, cover the whole with vinegar and water, and leave in a cool place for 3 days. Remove meat from the marinade and pat dry with kitchen paper. Heat fat in an ovenproof pot with lid and brown meat quickly all over, then add salt and rye bread. Gradually stir in vinegar liquid. Cover pot and place in oven for 1½ hours (gas mark 6/400°F/200°C). Remove joint and thicken the juices with cornflour blended with the water. Slice the meat and arrange on a platter. Serve the gravy separately.

Dumplings

Grüne Kartoffelklösse (Potato Dumplings)

1½ kg/3 lb potatoes	1 tsp salt
1 egg	croutons
60 g/2 oz/½ cup flour	

Boil half the potatoes in their jackets, peel while still hot and mash. Leave to cool, then rub them through a sieve. Peel and grate the remainder of the raw potatoes, place the pulp in a teatowel and squeeze out excess liquid. Combine the mash with the raw, grated potatoes. Add egg, flour and salt, and beat into a smooth paste. Form fist-sized dumplings. Press 4 or 5 croutons into the centre of each. Drop into a large pan of boiling water and simmer for about 20 minutes.

Semmelklösse (Bread Dumplings)

This recipe is economical and easy to prepare and goes well with Sauerbraten. Dumplings are immensely popular in Germany, and usually accompany meat dishes. They may be boiled, poached, fried or baked.

8 stale bread rolls	300 ml/½ pt/1 cup milk
half an onion, finely chopped	2 eggs
parsley, finely chopped	60 g/3 oz/½ cup flour
salt	1 tsp baking powder
50 g/2 oz/3 tbsp butter	

Quarter the bread rolls, and fry them with onion, parsley and salt in butter until golden brown. Place in a mixing bowl, cover with boiling milk and let this soak in. Add eggs, flour and baking powder, and work the whole into a soft dough. Shape fairly large dumplings and simmer them gently in salted water for 10 minutes.

Spätzle

Spätzle is an everyday pasta dish from Swabia, where it is eaten with almost any savoury dish. These little noodles are considered to be genuine only if made by hand.

---

450 g / 1 lb / 4 cups plain flour
3 eggs
½ tsp salt and enough liquid (half water, half milk) to form a very soft dough
1 tbsp butter for garnish

Sift flour, make a well in the middle and pour in eggs, beaten up with the salt. Starting from the middle, mix eggs into flour, gradually adding liquid until you have a very soft dough. Beat and knead the dough until it forms blisters. Place it onto a chopping board and scrape thin strips of dough straight into boiling, salted water with the broad side of a knife. Let them swell up for 3 minutes, fish them out with a sieve, rinse in hot water and place them in a serving bowl. Repeat until all the dough has been used up. Before serving, toss the Spätzle in browned butter.

Schnitzel

Though usually associated with Vienna, Schnitzel has a permanent place on the German bill of fare. In Holstein it is served with a fried egg as garnish, and in other parts of Germany cooks use mushrooms, sliced gherkins, or capers as garnish. I invite you to try one of the many variations.

4 veal cutlets	50 g/2 oz/4 tbsp fat
1 egg	150 ml/1/4 pt/1/2 cup stock
2 tbsp breadcrumbs	3 tbsp sour cream
salt and pepper	slices of lemon

Remove bones and tenderise cutlets with a meat hammer (or ask your butcher to do this for you). Beat the egg and season. Coat cutlets in beaten egg and then in breadcrumbs, and fry for 8-10 minutes on each side in very hot fat. Remove from pan. Pour the stock, mixed with sour cream, into the juices and boil for a couple of minutes. Pour this gravy over Schnitzels, decorate with lemon slices and serve with a salad and steamed parsley potatoes.

Krautwickel

Cabbage Rolls

These are fun to make and very popular with the family. The common cabbage is indispensable in Germany and this recipe will enhance its reputation elsewhere.

1 medium cabbage	2 eggs
2 potatoes, boiled	4 sprigs of parsley, chopped
500 g/1 lb lean minced beef (or	salt and pepper
half beef, half pork or lamb)	grated nutmeg
1 medium onion, finely	4 rashers smoked bacon
chopped	1 tbsp oil
1 tbsp breadcrumbs	600 ml/1 pt/2 cups stock

Separate the leaves of the cabbage, remove the stalk and wash leaves well. Blanch in boiling, salted water and allow to cool. Mix the minced meat with onion, breadcrumbs, eggs, parsley and seasoning. Mash the boiled potatoes and add to the meat mixture. Place a large spoonful of the mixture in a cabbage leaf, make a parcel and secure with wooden cocktail sticks. Repeat until mixture is used up. Chop and fry the bacon in oil in a pan, add cabbage rolls and stock. Cover pot and braise in oven for about 1 hour at gas mark 4/350°F/180°C. Remove sticks and serve cabbage rolls hot with potatoes or noodles.

Schweinebraten

Roast Pork

After this Bavarian Sunday lunch an afternoon nap is recommended! Pork is by far the most popular meat in Germany. I can remember when our local farmers killed their pigs we were presented with a Schlachtschüssel (slaughter bowl) placed clandestinely on our doorstep. The pot contained a deliciously roasted piece of pork, several blood- and liver-sausages and Sauerkraut, the whole covered with thick gravy.

1 kg/2½ lb loin pork	2 leeks
1 large onion	300 ml/½ pt/ 1 cup boiling
2 sticks celery	water

Seal meat by frying it on all sides in its own fat; then add diced onion, celery and leeks, and water. Cover pan and roast in medium oven for 2½ hours (gas mark 6/400°F/200°C). After 1 hour reduce the heat slightly and turn the meat to allow it to brown all over. When tender remove meat from the pan. Make a gravy by thickening the strained juices with cornflour or gravy browning.

Sauerkraut

Sauerkraut is surely the best known of German vegetable dishes. It is usually eaten with pork, though it can accompany all types of poultry and game. It is generally most practical to buy it ready-made, as making it at home is a lengthy process. It is manufactured in large quantities and left to mature for several weeks in a wooden tub in order to achieve its unique flavour. Good Sauerkraut should always be very white and juicy. Of the many ways of cooking it, this is my favourite.

500 g / 1 lb tin or jar of uncooked Sauerkraut	1 small apple
1 small onion	1 carrot
2 rashers of smoked bacon	1 (peeled) potato
2 tbsp oil	salt and pepper
	water

Rinse uncooked Sauerkraut thoroughly. Fry the diced onion and chopped bacon in 2 tbsp oil, add Sauerkraut, diced apple, grated carrot and grated raw potato. Season. Cover completely with water and boil for 1 hour.

Kasseler Rippchen

Cured Smoked Pork Ribs

This is the traditional accompaniment for Sauerkraut. One might even dub it the national dish of Germany. (There is no need for salt or pepper.)

1 kg / 2½ lb cured, smoked pork ribs (available at delicatessens)
1 large onion, sliced
2 tomatoes, peeled and chopped
1 large apple, peeled, cored and sliced
½ litre / 1 pt / 2 cups water
1 tbsp cornflour
150 ml / ¼ pt / ¾ cup sour cream

Place meat in a roasting dish, on a bed of onion, tomatoes and apple. Cover dish and bake in the oven for 30 minutes at gas mark 4 / 350°F / 180°C. Uncover, add half the water and roast for a further 2 hours. Remove the meat and rub the residue through a sieve. Make a sauce by stirring the cornflour and sour cream into the soft pulp and boil for about 2 minutes, then pour sauce over the ribs.

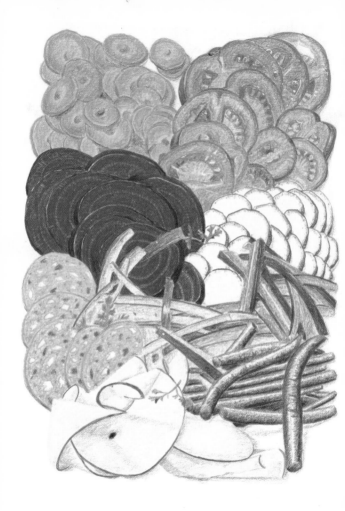

Salads

Kopfsalat mit Speck (Tom Thumb Lettuce with Bacon)

Wash the lettuce and separate the leaves. Arrange in a salad bowl. Fry about 50 g/2 oz diced bacon in olive oil until it is crisp. Add a little brown sugar and enough vinegar to make a dressing. Pour the hot dressing over the lettuce, and serve while the lettuce is still warm.

Fleischsalat (Meat Salad)

Sliced cooked potatoes, raw grated carrots and chopped apples form the basis of this salad. Add chopped cold meats (Wurst), mix with mayonnaise, sliced gherkins, chopped chives, and tomatoes.

Gemüsesalat (Vegetable Salad)

Try this dressing, which is suitable for all vegetable salads.

---

3 tbsp salad oil
1-2 tbsp wine vinegar or lemon juice
pinch of salt
a little sugar
finely chopped herbs (chives, dill)
1 small onion, finely chopped
celery salt or pepper as desired

Mix all the ingredients together thoroughly. Try dressing with any of the following vegetables (use 500 g/1 lb quantities): carrots (cut into thin discs, boil until just tender, drain and cool), runner beans (slice finely, boil until just tender, drain and cool), tomatoes (slice thinly), green or red peppers (core and slice thinly), cucumber (slice very thinly, omit onion from the dressing and replace with 2 tbsp of sour cream), beetroot (use boiled root, sliced very thinly), celeriac (boil until tender and slice very thinly).

Kartoffelsalat (Potato Salad)

1 kg/2½ lb potatoes	4 tbsp beef stock
1 onion, finely chopped	capers or anchovies
2 sweet/sour gherkins, roughly chopped	2 boiled eggs
	watercress
4 rashers streaky bacon	salt and pepper
4 tbsp vinegar	

Boil potatoes in their jackets until tender. Peel and slice them while still hot. Add onion, gherkins, chopped and crisply fried bacon, vinegar and beef stock. Season. Arrange in serving bowl and decorate with capers or anchovies, sliced boiled eggs and watercress. Allow to stand for a few hours.

Rotkohl (Red Cabbage)

Another salad which can be eaten hot or cold. It goes well with venison.

1 small onion	3 tbsp brown sugar
2 tbsp oil	4 tbsp wine vinegar
1 medium red cabbage	4 tbsp water
1 apple	salt
juice of half a lemon	pepper

Dice the onion and fry in the oil until crisp. Add the finely shredded cabbage, cored and diced apple, lemon juice, sugar, vinegar, water and seasoning. Stir well and place in a fireproof casserole. Cook in the oven at gas mark 3/325°F/160°C for 3 hours. Serve hot with a main meat dish or cold with a selection of cold meats.

Labskaus

Savoury Beef and Herrings with Potatoes and Eggs

This dish is local to Hamburg and Bremen. A traditional seafarer's meal, it is eaten at the launching of ships. Curiously, the name originates from the 18th-century English expression 'lob's course', meaning 'fool's meal'. It is, after all, a crazy combination of ingredients, but makes an exciting change from more conventional meals. Matjesherring is available in delicatessens.

500 g/1 lb pickled pork (or corned beef)	2 onions
2 Bismarck herrings	60 g/3 oz/5 tbsp cooking fat
2 gherkins	4 eggs
500 g/1 lb potatoes	1 Matjesherring
2 pickled beetroots	salt
	pepper

Boil the meat for 1 hour in the minimum possible quantity of water, then cut it into small cubes (if you use corned beef, just cut this into small chunks). Cut up the herrings, gherkins, beetroots and potatoes and fry the mixture in hot fat, add finely chopped onions, pour on the stock from the meat and steam for half an hour. Serve, arranged on lettuce leaves, topped with fried eggs and garnished with strips of Matjesherring.

Rehblatt

Roast Shoulder of Venison

Venison has always been popular in the densely forested areas of middle and southern Germany, but nowadays it is appreciated much more widely. Low in fats and rich in albumen, it is very tasty, though a little on the dry side. The meat should therefore be covered with rashers of smoked bacon while cooking. A glass of brandy poured over the joint just before it goes into the oven enhances the flavour and creates a mouthwatering aroma.

---

1 kg/2½ lb venison (shoulder cut)
300 ml/½ pt/1 cup buttermilk
250 g/8 oz streaky smoked bacon
50 g/2 oz/4 tbsp fat or oil
salt
1 small onion
300 ml/½ pt/1 cup water
1 glass brandy

Soak the meat in buttermilk for 3 days, then wrap it in bacon, place in the hot fat and seal on all sides. Sprinkle with a little salt. Slice onion and soften with the meat. Add water and brandy, cover pot and steam-roast in the oven at gas mark 4/350°F/180°C for 2 hours. Serve with red cabbage and parsley potatoes.

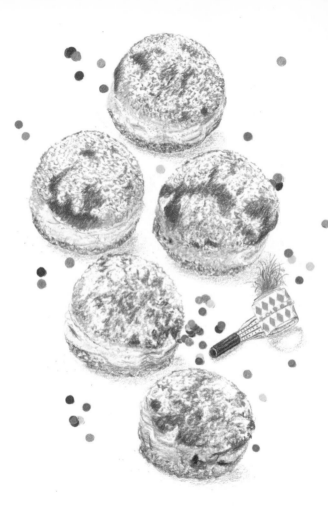

Fastnachtsküchlein

Carnival Doughnuts

On the 11th day of the 11th month at 11.11 a.m. the Karneval starts in Cologne. It gradually spreads to the rest of the country, with each region organising its own zany jollifications for this pre-Lenten festival. In Southern Germany the Küchlein is the traditional Fasching, or Fastnacht, fare.

20 g/1 oz baker's yeast (or dried yeast)	75 g/3 oz/³⁄₈ cup melted butter
150 ml/1¼ pt/½ cup warm milk	50 g/2 oz/¼ cup sugar
500 g/1 lb/4½ cups plain flour	pinch of salt
1 egg	oil for deep-frying
	caster sugar

Dissolve the yeast in the milk in a large bowl, cover with 100 g/4 oz/1 cup of the flour. Stand in a warm place, and leave to rise for about ½ hour. Add the melted butter, beaten egg, sugar, salt and the rest of the flour, and beat and knead to a soft, smooth dough. Leave again in a warm place to rise to double its size. Turn onto a floured board and roll out to a 1-inch/2-cm thickness. Use a wine glass to cut out rounds, or use your baking wheel and divide dough into 3-inch squares. Leave these once more to rise until the dough forms tiny blisters when poked with the handle of a wooden spoon. Lower the doughnuts into boiling oil for about 4 minutes on each side, or until golden brown all over, then remove them with a draining spoon. Place them on kitchen paper to drain off the surplus fat. Roll in caster sugar and serve while still warm.

Heidelbeerkompott

Bilberry Dessert

Fruits from the forest are always a welcome change from the more exotic variety. My mother and I spent many happy hours in the tranquil pine forests of Franconia, picking bilberries, wild raspberries and strawberries, and turning them into delicious desserts.

---

500 g / 1 lb fresh bilberries
3 heaped tbsp sugar

Place the berries in a bowl, cover with sugar and leave until they have absorbed it. Cook very slowly on a low heat until the fruit is soft. This method can be used for other types of soft fruit.

Apfelmus

Apple Purée

For this delicious dessert you can use windfalls. There is no need to peel them. Add cinnamon and cloves for a spicier version.

---

1 kg / 2½ lb apples
150 ml / ¼ pt / ½ cup water
3 heaped tbsp sugar

Cut the apples into small wedges, add the water and simmer gently until the fruit is soft. Rub through a sieve and add sugar to taste. If you like, add a handful of stoned raisins and chopped almonds. Place the purée in a glass bowl and serve chilled with whipped cream, or as an accompaniment to potato cakes.

Frankfurter Kranz

Frankfurt Ring

For the best results, spoil yourself and your guests and use butter in this recipe.

100 g/4 oz/1 cup butter or margarine	4 drops lemon essence or 1 tbsp rum
150 g/6 oz/¾ cup caster sugar	150 g/6 oz/1½ cup plain flour
3 eggs	50 g/2 oz/5 tbsp cornflour
salt	2 tbsp baking powder

Filling

2 tbsp custard powder	250 g/8 oz/1 cup butter
300 ml/½ pt/1 cup milk	

Cream butter and sugar until light and fluffy and gradually stir in eggs, lemon essence or rum, with a pinch of salt. Sift together the flour, cornflour and baking powder and gradually add to the butter mixture. Spoon into a greased, ring-shaped mould (24 cm/10 in diameter) and bake at gas mark 4/350°F/180°C for 50 minutes.

For the filling, make a thick custard and let it cool. Cream the butter and mix it with the custard. To avoid curdling ensure that both custard and butter have the same temperature.

Prepare a crunchy coating by melting together 50 g/2 oz/¼ cup sugar and ½ tsp butter and stir until golden brown. Add 100 g/4 oz/1 cup chopped almonds or hazelnuts and pour the whole on to greaseproof paper. When cool, break into small pieces.

When the cake is cool enough cut through it twice, creating three layers, and spread filling on each layer. Cover the cake with the rest of the buttercream and sprinkle the whole lavishly with the toffee mixture. This cake tastes best the next day.

Apfelkuchen mit Sahne

Applecake with Whipped Cream

This is a wonderful cake. It reigns supreme in Germany's coffee houses and is easily reproduced in your own kitchen.

125 g/5 oz/¾ cup butter	salt
125 g/5 oz/¾ cup caster sugar	200 g/7 oz/1½ cup plain flour
3 eggs	1 heaped tsp baking powder
½ tsp lemon essence	1-3 tbsp milk

Topping

3 large apples	2 tbsp hot water
juice of ½ lemon	2 tbsp apricot jam
sugar	300 ml/½ pt/1 cup whipping cream
1 tsp gelatine powder	

Cream the butter and sugar until light and fluffy. Add eggs one by one, lemon essence and a pinch of salt. Sift the flour and baking powder together and stir into the mixture gradually, adding milk as necessary. When the milk drops heavily off the spoon, pour it into a well-greased springform (26 cm/10 in diameter with a detachable base). Peel and cut the apples into thin wedges, toss them in lemon juice and arrange them in a circular pattern on top of the cake. Sprinkle with sugar and bake for 45 minutes at gas mark 4/350°F/180°C. In the meantime make an apricot glaze by dissolving the gelatine in the hot water and stirring in the apricot jam. Brush glaze over the baked cake while it is still hot. When cool serve with whipped cream.

Nürnberger Lebkuchen

Nürnberg Gingerbread

Nürnberg, noted for its heritage of art and architecture, is also famous for its Christmas market and gingerbread. This recipe from the Middle Ages received its name – Lebkuchen, or 'cake of life' from the natural ingredients and spices it uses, which were considered to possess life-sustaining and stimulating qualities. At Christmas, a gingerbread house is a firm favourite with young and old, and who knows, it may have been a passion for Lebkuchen that inspired the Brothers Grimm to write the tale *Hansel and Gretel*.

350 g/¾ lb honey	250 g/8 oz/ 2 cups chopped
150 g/6 oz/¾ cup caster	almonds
sugar	½ tsp ground cloves
750 g/1½ lb/6½ cups flour	½ tsp ground cinnamon
pinch baking soda	½ tsp ground ginger
1 tsp baking powder	150 g/6 oz/1 cup mixed peel

Bring the honey, with half the sugar, to boiling point, and keep boiling until it drops in beads from the spoon. Leave to cool, then pour it over the sieved flour. Add the baking powder and baking soda. Knead to a smooth dough and leave for two days in a cool place. Boil the remaining sugar with a little water to a syrup. Quickly sauté the almonds in this. Blend the syrup and almonds into the dough as quickly as possible, adding the spices. Roll out the dough (about 1 cm thick) on a floured board. Cut into biscuit-sized oblongs with a sharp knife, sprinkle with the chopped peel and leave in a warm place for a day. Finally bake in a hot oven, gas mark 7/425°F/220°C, for 25 minutes. Remove from oven and while still warm brush with a sugar glaze.

Echter Dresdner Weinachtsstollen

Dresden Christmas Loaf

Each region of Germany boasts its own distinctive recipe for the main Yuletide fare. This Christmas bread has been made in Saxony since the 15th century and is considered to be one of the most delicious.

150 g/5 oz yeast	250 g/8 oz/2 cups chopped almonds
250 g/8 oz/1 cup sugar	
150 ml/¼ pt/½ cup milk	250 g/8 oz/1½ cups mixed peel
1 kg/2 lb/8 cups self-raising flour	juice of ½ lemon
500 g/1 lb/2 cups melted butter	1 small glass rum
2 tbsp vanilla sugar	pinch of salt

Decoration
25 g/1 oz/2 tbsp butter
icing (confectioners') sugar

Mix the yeast, a little of the sugar and 5 tbsp of the warm milk in a jug. Sift the flour into a bowl and make a well in the centre. Pour in the yeast mixture and cover it with a thin layer of flour. Leave to stand for a few minutes; then add the other ingredients as well as the remainder of the milk, and knead into a smooth dough. Tear the dough apart and again knead it for a few minutes until air bubbles appear. When really soft and pliable let the dough stand for 2 hours in a warm place, covered with a teatowel. Halve the dough and roll out each piece into a 4 cm thick oblong; fold the long side over once. Place both loaves on a greased baking tray and bake for 60 minutes in a medium oven (gas mark 4/350°F/180°C). Remove from oven and while still warm brush with melted butter and dust with icing sugar.

Christbaumgebäck

Christmas Tree Biscuits

These make excellent decorations, especially when they have been decorated with different-coloured icings. Choose Christmassy biscuit cutters, shaped like stars, bells and angels. These biscuits are really fun to make and the children can help with tying on the strings.

---

4 eggs
250 g/8 oz/1 cup sugar
500 g/1 lb/4 cups flour

Cream the eggs and sugar for 10 to 15 minutes. Add the flour. Roll out the dough on a floured board, and cut into shapes using pastry cutters (don't forget to make the small hole needed for the ties). Brush with beaten egg yolk and bake biscuits in the oven at gas mark 7/425°F/220°C for 10 minutes.

Blau Karpfen

Blue Carp

Carp is the traditional Christmas Eve dish, and is cooked 'blue'. The fish is not scaled, so that everyone can save one scale to bring them luck throughout the coming year. The fish's blue shimmer is a German speciality and is achieved by scalding the fish with boiling wine vinegar and leaving it to stand in a draught.

1 large carp	*a few peppercorns*
salt	*1 tbsp dried herbs*
½ litre/1 pt/2 cups wine	*creamed horseradish*
vinegar	*2 oz butter*
1 onion	

Place carp in a large pan, rub in some salt, and pour boiling wine vinegar over it. Leave in a draught for a few minutes. Bring to the boil in the same pan and add sliced onions, peppercorns and herbs. Cover and place in oven at medium heat (gas mark 4/350°F/180°C) for 30 minutes or until cooked. Rinse the fish quickly, first in hot water, then in cold. Return it to the stock for long enough to reheat. Place fish on hot platter, pour browned butter over it and serve with creamed horseradish.

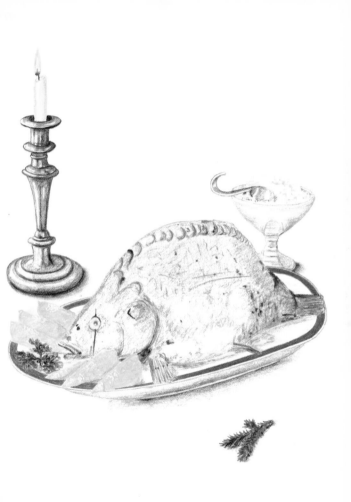

Drinks

Man learns first how to drink. Later, he learns how to eat. He should therefore be thankful, and never forget how to drink.

In Germany wine is much appreciated, and so is beer, and indeed schnaps. Each has its place on the table and according to taste and convention is consumed regularly with enjoyment. There are many fine wines to choose from. Hock comes from the four main areas round the river Rhine: Koblenz-Rheingau, Rheinhessen, the Nahe and the Palatinate. Wines from the four areas have very different characters and flavours. Then there are the Moselle wines, made from grapes which grow on the hills alongside the rivers Moselle, Ruhr and Saar. These wines should be drunk young and chilled. Franconian wines, from areas around Würzburg, are becoming more popular. Here are some of the most renowned German wines. Hock: Liebfraumilch, Rüdesheimer Rosengarten, Niersteiner Domthal. Moselle: Berncasteler, Piesporter.

We mustn't forget the German Sekt or champagne – Cabinet Deinhard and Henkell, to name but two. They say that if you drink a small bottle of Sekt a day you will live to a ripe old age.

Like the wines, the many varieties of beers and lagers will help make your meal a complete success.

Schnaps, originally made by monks, who distilled it for medicinal purposes, has been produced for centuries. It is made from fruit, mainly cherries, plums or pears, and is still considered a remedy for biliousness.

Neujahrspunsch

New Year's Punch

In Germany New Year's Eve goes with a bang, literally. Every town and village organises its own fireworks display starting at the stroke of midnight and accompanied by the glorious sound of church bells ringing in the New Year. Afterwards the revellers relax with this heart-warming drink.

150 ml/¼ pt/½ cup water	3 heaped tbsp sugar
1 cinnamon stick	1 litre bottle full-bodied red
4 cloves	wine
peel of ½ lemon	½ bottle of rum

Boil the water and simmer for 5 minutes with the spices, sugar and lemon peel, add wine and rum and reheat to nearly boiling point. Remove spices and serve in warmed glasses. Decorate with thin slices of lemon.

Sektbowle

Champagne Cup

This refreshing drink is ideal for your summer party on the lawn.

500 g/1 lb fresh fruit (strawberries, peaches, pineapple)
100 g/4 oz/½ cup sugar
1 bottle white wine
1 bottle Sekt

Clean and slice the fruit, place it in a bowl and cover it with sugar and a glass of wine. Keep tightly covered for 2 hours in the fridge, then pour in the remainder of the wine and Sekt, both chilled. *Prosit!*

Index